Ritual Lighting

Ritual Lighting

Carol Ann Duffy

with artwork by Stephen Raw

PICADOR

First published 2014 by Picador
an imprint of Pan Macmillan, a division of Macmillan Publishers Limited
Pan Macmillan, 20 New Wharf Road, London N1 9RR
Basingstoke and Oxford
Associated companies throughout the world
www.panmacmillan.com

ISBN 978-1-4472-7450-6

1 3 5 7 9 8 6 4 2

A CIP catalogue record for this book is available from the British Library.

Printed and bound by CPI Group (UK) Ltd, Croydon, CR0 4YY

Visit www.picador.com to read more about all our books
and to buy them. You will also find features, author interviews and
news of any author events, and you can sign up for e-newsletters
so that you're always first to hear about our new releases.

Contents

ACKNOWLEDGEMENTS

With thanks to Matthew Hollis, Kris Doyle, Paul Baggaley, Peter Straus, Jane Roberts, Theresa-Mary Morton, Graham and Betty Hines, and Nia Dryhurst.

PUBLISHER'S NOTE

Ritual Lighting is published to coincide with the exhibition 'Poetry for the Palace: Poets Laureate from Dryden to Duffy', showing at The Queen's Gallery, Palace of Holyroodhouse in 2014. The first of its kind, the exhibition contains previously unseen manuscripts from the Royal Collection and reveals the changing nature of the Laureateship over 350 years. The textual artist Stephen Raw – who is concerned with 'making language visible' – has collaborated with Carol Ann Duffy on many of her public commissions and his work with her forms part of the exhibition. Notes on both poems and artwork are included at the back of this book.

Love's
light,
a fluent
tongue,

Chaucer's Valentine

for Nia

The lyf so short, the craft so long to lerne . . .
but be my valentine
                        and I'll one candle burn,
love's light a fluent tongue,
old habit young, the door ajar
to where our bed awaits,
                           not in a room
but in a wood, all thrilled with birds,
the flight of early English words to verse,
there as sweetness evermore now is,
this human kiss,
                  love's written bliss in every age . . .
hold the front page.

At Jerez

Who wouldn't feel favoured,
at the end of a week's labour,
to receive as part-wages
a pale wine
that puts the mouth in mind of the sea . . .

and not gladly be kissed
by gentle William Shakespeare's lips,
the dark, raisiny taste of his song;
bequeathed to his thousand daughters and sons,
the stolen wines of the Spanish sun . . .

then walk the cool bodegas' aisles –
where flor and oxygen
grow talented in fragrances and flavours –
to sniff, sip, spit, swallow, savour . . .

See lines and lines of british boys rewind
Back to their Trenches,
kiss the photographs from home—
MOTHERS, SWEETHEARTS,
SISTERS,
YOUNGER BROTHERS NOT ENTERING
the story now
TO DIE
and DIE
and DIE.
DULCE-NO-
DECORUM-NO
-PRO PATRIA
MORT.
YOU Walk Away.
YOU Walk Away; drop your gun (FIXED BAYONET)
LIKE all your mates do too—
HARRY, TOMMY,
WILFRED,
EDWARD, BERT- and Light a
cigarette.

Last Post

In all my dreams, before my helpless sight,
He plunges at me, guttering, choking, drowning.

If poetry could tell it backwards, true, begin
that moment shrapnel scythed you to the stinking mud . . .
but you get up, amazed, watch bled bad blood
run upwards from the slime into its wounds;
see lines and lines of British boys rewind
back to their trenches, kiss the photographs from home –
mothers, sweethearts, sisters, younger brothers
not entering the story now
to die and die and die.
Dulce – No – Decorum – No – Pro patria mori.
You walk away.

You walk away; drop your gun (fixed bayonet)
like all your mates do too –
Harry, Tommy, Wilfred, Edward, Bert –
and light a cigarette.
There's coffee in the square,
warm French bread,
and all those thousands dead
are shaking dried mud from their hair
and queueing up for home. Freshly alive,
a lad plays Tipperary to the crowd, released
from History; the glistening, healthy horses fit for heroes, kings.

You lean against a wall,
your several million lives still possible
and crammed with love, work, children, talent, English beer, good food.
You see the poet tuck away his pocket-book and smile.

If poetry could truly tell it backwards,
then it would.

The Pendle Witches

One voice for ten dragged this way once
by superstition, ignorance.
Thou shalt not suffer a witch to live.

Witch: female, cunning, manless, old,
daughter of such, of evil faith;
in the murk of Pendle Hill, a crone.

Here, heavy storm-clouds, ill-will brewed,
over fields, fells, farms, blighted woods.
On the wind's breath, curse of crow and rook.

From poverty, no poetry
but weird spells, half-prayer, half-threat;
sharp pins in little dolls of death.

At daylight's gate, the things we fear
darken and form. That tree, that rock,
a slattern's shape ropes the devil's dog.

Something upholds us in its palm —
landscape, history, sudden time —
and, above, the gormless witness moon

below which Demdike, Chattox, shrieked,
like hags, unloved, an underclass,
eyes red, gobs gummed, unwell, unfed.

But that was then — when difference
made ghouls of neighbours; children begged,
foul, feral, filthy, in their cowls.

Grim skies, the grey remorse of rain;
cloudbreak, sunset's shame; four seasons,
turning centuries, in Lancashire,

away from Castle, Jury, Judge,
huge crowd, rough rope, short drop, no grave;
only future tourists who might grieve.

OVER FIELDS,
FELLS, FARMS,
BLIGHTED WOODS.

THE CATHE...
TOLLED, COULD N...
NOR THE LIVER BIR...
OR THE MERS...
IN NO LANGUAGE FOR THE SLANDE...

NOT THE RAW, RED THROAT...
OR THE COPS'...
NOT THE CLOCK, SLOW HANDCL...
OR THE MEM...
OR THE TABLOID...

BUT FATHERS TOLD OF THEIR DA...
ON THE LIPS OF...
HONOURED FOR BITTER YEARS BY OR...
NOT A MATTER OF FOO...

OVER THIS GRE...
TRUTH, THE SWE...

AL BELL,

R TELL;

NUTE IN THEIR STONE SPELL;

THOUGH SEAGULLS WAILED, CURSED,

DEAD... OVERHEAD,

KOP, KEENING,

S, CENSORED OF MEANING;

1G TH CORONER'S DEADLINE,

THATCHER,

LINE...

ERS; THE NAMES OF SONS

MOTHERS WERE PRAYERS; LOST ONES

AN, COUSIN, WIFE -

LL, BUT P LIFE.

CITY, LIGHT AFTER
LONG DARK; AND
SILVER SONG
LARK.

Liverpool

The Cathedral bell, tolled, could never tell;
nor the Liver Birds, mute in their stone spell;
or the Mersey, though seagulls wailed, cursed, overhead,
in no language for the slandered dead . . .

not the raw, red throat of the Kop, keening,
or the cops' words, censored of meaning;
not the clock, slow handclapping the coroner's deadline,
or the memo to Thatcher, or the tabloid headline . . .

but fathers told of their daughters; the names of sons
on the lips of their mothers were prayers; lost ones
honoured for bitter years by orphan, cousin, wife –
not a matter of football, but of life.

Over this great city, light after long dark;
and truth, the sweet silver song of a lark.

Birmingham

for Tariq Jahan

After the evening prayers at the mosque,
came the looters in masks,
                              and you three stood,
beloved in your neighbourhood,
brave, bright, brothers,
to be who you were –
a hafiz is one who has memorised
the entire Koran;
                    a devout man –
then the lout in the speeding car
who purposefully mounted the kerb . . .

I think we all should kneel
                              on that English street,
where he widowed your pregnant wife, Shazad,
tossed your soul to the air, Abdul,
and brought your father, Haroon, to his knees,
his face masked in your blood
on the rolling news
where nobody's children riot and burn.

BELO
in
NEIGHBO
BRAVE
BTO

VER

YOUR

OURHOOO,

BRIGHT,

HERS

White Cliffs

Worth their salt, England's white cliffs;
a glittering breastplate
Caesar saw from his ship;
the sea's gift to the land,
where samphire-pickers hung from their long ropes,
gathering, under a gull-glad sky,
in Shakespeare's mind's eye; astonishing
in Arnold's glimmering verse;
marvellous geology, geography;
to time, deference; war, defence;
first view or last of here, home,
in painting, poem, play, in song;
something fair and strong implied in chalk,
what we might wish ourselves.

Philharmonic

Wounds in wood, where the wind grieves
in slow breves,
                    or a breeze
hovers and heals; brass,
                    bold as itself,
alchemical, blowing breath to blared gold;
all strings attached to silver sound.
This the composer found
                    in his deaf joy, despair,
and the brilliant boy; a where for time and space;
a place in endless air for perfect art –
a songbird's flight
                    through a great medieval hall
over the dancing dead.

WOUNDS
IN WOOD,
WHERE
THE WIND
GRIEVES
IN SLOW
BREVES

The Beauty of the Church

Look, you are beautiful, beloved;
your eyes, framed by your hair,
are birds in the leaves of a tree,
doves in the Cedar of Lebanon;
your hair shines, a stream in sunlight
tumbling from the mountain; you are fair,
loved; your mouth, entrance; your kiss, key;
your lips, soft scarlet, opening;
your tongue, wine-sweet; your teeth, new lambs
in the pastures; your voice is for psalm, song.

I see your face; I say your face
is the garden where I sought love;
my head filled with dew; my hands
sweet with myrrh; my naked feet
in wet grasses; my mouth honey-smeared.
Your voice called at the door of my heart.

I am sick with love.
Turn away your eyes from mine,
they have overcome me.
You have ravished my heart with your eyes.
You have kissed me with the kisses of your mouth
in our green bed, under the beams of cedar,
the rafters of fir.
You are altogether lovely.
Your cheeks, spices and sweet flowers;
your breath, camphire and spikenard;
saffron; calamus and cinnamon;
frankincense and aloes;
your throat is for pearls;
your two breasts are honey and milk;
your left hand should be under my head,
your right hand embracing me.
Just to look at your hand,
I am sick with love.

You are the apple tree among the trees of the forest.
I lie under your shadow
and your fruit is sweet to my taste.
You are a cluster of camphire in the vineyards;
an orchard of ripe figs, pomegranates.
I am yours and you are mine,
until the day breaks and shadows fade.
No river to quench love, no sea to drown it.

I was in your eyes and I found favour.
I was all you desired and I gave you my loves.

I say the roof of your mouth is the best wine;
you are rose, lily, a cluster of grapes.
I looked for you at night on my bed.
I rose and walked the city streets,
searching for you.
I found you. I held you
and would not let you go,
until I had brought you to the field,
where we lay,
circled by the roes and hinds of the meadows.

I rose up to open to you
and your hands smelled of myrrh.
Your navel, a goblet which needed no wine.
How beautiful your feet.
The joints of your thighs were jewels.
Your knees were apples.

I sleep, but my heart wakes to your whisper.
You have brought me to this bed
and your banner over me is love.
Set me as a seal, beloved,
for love is strong as death,
set me as a seal upon your heart.

SHAKESPEARE
SMALL LATIN
and LESS GREEK,
ALL English
yours,

dear LAD,
Local,
word-BLESSED,
LANGUAGE
loved BEST;

the LIVING
human
MUSIC
on our TONGUES,
YOUNG,
OLD,
who we were
OR WILL BE,
history's SHADOW,

Love's will,
our heart's
iambic BEAT,
Brother
Through
time;?
full-rhyme
To us.

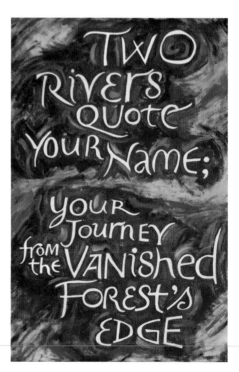

TWO
RIVERS
QUOTE
YOUR NAME;

your
Journey
from the VANISHED
FOREST'S
EDGE

Shakespeare

Small Latin and less Greek, all English yours,
dear lad, local, word-blessed, language loved best;
the living human music on our tongues,
young, old, who we were or will be, history's shadow,
love's will, our heart's iambic beat, brother
through time; full-rhyme to us.
                                    Two rivers quote your name;
your journey from the vanished forest's edge
to endless fame – a thousand written souls,
pilgrims, redeemed in poetry – ends here, begins again.
And so, you knew this well, you do not die –
courtier, countryman, noter of flowers and bees,
war's laureate, magician, Janus-faced –
but make a great Cathedral, genius, of this place.

Pathway

I saw my father walking in my garden
and where he walked,
                              the garden lengthened
to a changing mile
which held all seasons of the year.
He did not see me, staring from my window,
a child's star face, hurt light from stricken time,
and he had treaded spring and summer grasses
before I thought to stir, follow him.

Autumn's cathedral, open to the weather, rose
high above, flawed amber, gorgeous ruin; his shadow
stretched before me, *cappa magna*,
my own, obedient, trailed like a nun.
He did not turn. I heard the rosaries of birds.
The trees, huge doors, swung open and I knelt.

He stepped into a silver room of cold;
a narrow bed of ice stood glittering,
and though my father wept, he could not leave,
but had to strip, then shiver in his shroud,

till winter palmed his eyes for frozen bulbs,
or sliced his tongue, a silencing of worms.

The moon a simple headstone without words.

the
MOON
a SIMPLE
HEADSTONE
WITHOUT
WORDS

I SAW Love's child
uttered,
unborn, only by rain,
then and now,
all future past,
an unseen.

Has forever been then?
Yes,
forever has been.

An Unseen

I watched love leave, turn, wave, want not to go,
depart, return;
late spring, a warm slow blue of air, old-new.
Love was here; not; missing, love was there;
each look, first, last.

Down the quiet road, away, away, towards
the dying time,
love went, brave soldier, the song dwindling;
walked to the edge of absence; all moments going,
gone; bells through rain

to fall on the carved names of the lost. I saw
love's child uttered,
unborn, only by rain, then and now, all future
past, an unseen. Has forever been then? Yes,
forever has been.

Silver Lining

Five miles up, the hush and shoosh of ash,
yet the sky is as clean as a wiped slate –
I could write my childhood there. Selfish
to sit in this garden, listening to the past –
a Tudor bee wooing its flower, a lawnmower –
when grounded planes mean ruined plans, holidays
on hold, sore absences from weddings, funerals,
wingless commerce.
                         But Britain's birds
sing in this spring, from Inverness to Liverpool,
from Crieff, Caernarfon, Cambridge, Wenlock Edge,
Land's End to John O'Groats; the music silence summons,
George Herbert heard, Burns, Edward Thomas; briefly, us.

THE MUSIC
SILENCE
SUMMONS,
George Herbert
Heard,
Burns,
Edward Thomas;
Briefly, us.

THE CROWN TRANSLATES a WOMAN to a QUEEN — ENDLESS GOLD, circling itself, AN LIKE A WELL.

fathomless, FOR THE YEARS to DROWN IN — History's BRIDE, ANOINTED, blessed, for a CROWNING.

ONE HEAD ALONE CAN KNOW ITS WEIGHT, on THRONE, in PAGEANTRY, AND FEEL IT STILL, in private SPACE, WHEN IT'S LIFTED:

Not A hollow THING, but A MEASURING; NO halo, TREASURE, but A VALUING; DECADES A DUTY. Time-gifted, the CROWN IS OLD LIGHT,

JOURNEYING FROM SKULLS of KINGS to LIVING QUEEN.   ITS JEWELS GLOW, VIRTUES:

LOYALTY'S RUBY, blood-deep; SAPPHIRE'S ICE RESILIENCE; EMERALD EVERGREEN; the SLY PEARL HUMILITY.

MY WHOLE LIFE, WHETHER IT BE LONG OR SHORT, DEVOTED TO YOUR SERVICE. NOT Lightly WORN.

The Crown

The crown translates a woman to a Queen —
endless gold, circling itself, an O like a well,
fathomless, for the years to drown in — history's bride,
anointed, blessed, for a crowning. One head alone
can know its weight, on throne, in pageantry,
and feel it still, in private space, when it's lifted:
not a hollow thing, but a measuring; no halo,
treasure, but a valuing; decades and duty. Time-gifted,
the crown is old light, journeying from skulls of kings
to living Queen.
        Its jewels glow, virtues; loyalty's ruby,
blood-deep; sapphire's ice resilience; emerald evergreen;
the shy pearl, humility. My whole life, whether it be long
or short, devoted to your service. Not lightly worn.

Lessons in the Orchard

An apple's soft thump on the grass, somewhen
in this place. What was it? Beauty of Bath.
What was it? Yellow, vermillion, round, big, splendid;
already escaping the edge of itself,
                                        like the mantra of bees,
like the notes of rosemary, tarragon, thyme.
Poppies scumble their colour onto the air,
now and there, here, then and again.

                                Alive-alive-oh,
the heart's impulse to cherish; thus,
a woman petalling paint onto a plate –
cornflower blue –
as the years pressed out her own violet ghost;
that slow brush of vanishing cloud on the sky.

And the dragonfly's talent for turquoise.
And the goldfish art of the pond.
And the open windows calling the garden in.

This bowl, life, that we fill and fill.

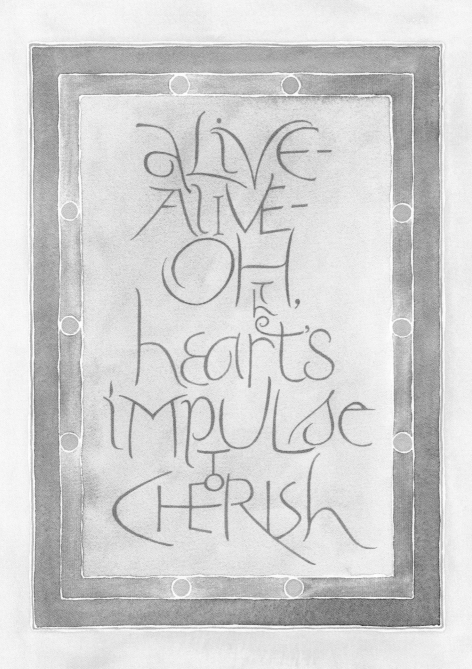

SNOW

Mind of

SIFTING

Drafting

YEAR'S

WAS THE
TIME,
ITSELF,
THE OLD
ENDS.

Christmas Eve

for Ella

Time was slow snow sieved by the night,
a kind of love from the blurred moon;
your small town swooning, unabashed,
was Winter's own.

Snow was the mind of Time, sifting
itself, drafting the old year's end.
You wrote your name on the window-pane
with your young hand.

And your wishes went up in smoke,
beyond where a streetlamp studied
the thoughtful snow on Christmas Eve,
beyond belief,

as Time, snow, darkness, child, kindled.
Downstairs, the ritual lighting of the candles.

NOTES ON THE POEMS AND ARTWORK

'Chaucer's Valentine' was commissioned by the *Guardian* and published on the masthead on 14 February 2013.

PRESSED TERRACOTTA CLAY, BISQUE-FIRED. Fourteen tiles, each 250 X 300 MM.

'At Jerez' was written in 2009 for the 'Laureate's Choice' sherry label. The tradition of giving sherry to the Poet Laureate began in 1619 but was discontinued from 1790 until 1986, when it was revived by the Sherry Institute of Spain for Ted Hughes.

WATERCOLOUR AND GOUACHE. 370 X 450 MM.

'Last Post' was commissioned by the BBC and read at the Armistice Day Service at Westminster Abbey in 2009.

GICLÉE PRINT. 320 X 480 MM.

'The Pendle Witches' was commissioned in 2012 for the Lancashire Witches Walk. Each of the poem's ten tercets is displayed on a cast-iron waymarker, set at intervals along the witches' path from Pendle to Lancaster.

WATERCOLOUR. 600 X 130 MM.

'Liverpool' was written after the publication of the Hillsborough Report in 2012.

WATERCOLOUR. 640 X 460 MM.

'Birmingham' was written in August 2011, after the riots in Winson Green.

CHINESE STICK INK ON WATERCOLOUR PAPER. 480 X 320 MM.

'White Cliffs' was commissioned by the National Trust in 2012 to mark the purchase, through public appeal, of one of the last stretches of this landmark.

MACHINE-CUT 640 GSM SAUNDERS WATERFORD PAPER, MOUNTED ON THE SAME. 2840 MM X 1340 MM.

'Philharmonic' was commissioned by the Royal Philharmonic Society to celebrate its bicentenary in 2013.

CHINESE STICK INK ON WATERCOLOUR PAPER. 230 X 300 MM.

'**The Beauty of the Church**' was written for the Bush Theatre's *Sixty-Six Books* project on the 400th anniversary of the King James Bible in 2011.

CHINESE STICK INK ON WATERCOLOUR PAPER. 560 X 210 MM.

'**Shakespeare**' was commissioned by the Royal Shakespeare Company in November 2012 to mark the end of the World Shakespeare Festival.

ACRYLIC ON WATERCOLOUR PAPER, MOUNTED ON BOARD. The seven original panels hang in the Swan Theatre, Stratford-upon-Avon. Each panel is 600 X 1000 MM.

'**Pathway**' was written on the death of the poet's father in Stafford in 2011. He had been placed on the subsequently discredited Liverpool Care Pathway.

INK DRAWING. 200 X 200 MM.

'**An Unseen**' was written for *1914: Poetry Remembers* (Faber, 2013, ed. Duffy) in response to Wilfred Owen's 'The Send-off'.

WATERCOLOUR. 340 X 420 MM.

'**Silver Lining**' was commissioned by the BBC's *Today* programme in April 2010 during the volcano ash disaster.

CHINESE STICK INK ON WATERCOLOUR PAPER. 230 X 300 MM.

'**The Crown**' was commissioned by Westminster Abbey for the 60th Anniversary of the Coronation of Queen Elizabeth II in 2013.

WATERCOLOUR AND MASKING FLUID. 1000 X 1300 MM. A print of this artwork was wrapped around a three-metre-high column for display in the exhibition.

'**Lessons in the Orchard**' was written in 2014 to celebrate the 25th anniversary of the Charleston Festival, held at the home of Duncan Grant and Vanessa Bell.

WATERCOLOUR AND GOUACHE ON WATERCOLOUR PAPER. 290 X 380 MM.

'**Christmas Eve**' was written for *The Twelve Poems of Christmas*, edited by Carol Ann Duffy in each year of her Laureateship to support Candlestick Press.

WATERCOLOUR. 400 X 200 MM.

Prints of the artwork in this book are available, please go to
www.stephenraw.com *or* **www.picador.com** *to find out more.*